I0425861

January 2012

CHEMICAL, BIOLOGICAL, RADIOLOGICAL, AND NUCLEAR RISK ASSESSMENTS

DHS Should Establish More Specific Guidance for Their Use

GAO

Accountability * Integrity * Reliability

GAO-12-272

CHEMICAL, BIOLOGICAL, RADIOLOGICAL, AND NUCLEAR RISK ASSESSMENTS

DHS Should Establish More Specific Guidance for Their Use

Highlights of GAO-12-272, a report to the Committee on Homeland Security and Governmental Affairs, U.S. Senate

Why GAO Did This Study

The 2001 anthrax attacks in the United States highlighted the need to develop response plans and capabilities to protect U.S. citizens from chemical, biological, radiological, and nuclear (CBRN) agents. Since 2004, the Department of Homeland Security (DHS) has spent at least $70 million developing more than 20 CBRN risk assessments. GAO was requested to assess, from fiscal year 2004 to the present, the extent to which DHS has used its CBRN risk assessments to inform CBRN response plans and CBRN capabilities, and has institutionalized their use. GAO examined relevant laws, Homeland Security Presidential Directives, an Executive Order, DHS guidance, and all 12 relevant interagency CBRN response plans developed by DHS. Based on a review of a United States governmentwide CBRN database and DHS interviews, among other things, GAO selected a nongeneralizable set of seven DHS capabilities used specifically for detecting or responding to CBRN incidents to identify examples of DHS's use of its CBRN risk assessments. GAO also interviewed relevant DHS officials. This is a public version of a classified report that GAO issued in October 2011. Information DHS deemed sensitive or classified has been redacted.

What GAO Recommends

GAO recommends that DHS develop more specific guidance, including written procedures, that details when and how DHS components should consider using the department's CBRN risk assessments to inform related response planning efforts and capability investment decision making. DHS agreed with the recommendation.

View GAO-12-272. For more information, contact William O. Jenkins, Jr. at (202) 512-8777 or jenkinswo@gao.gov.

What GAO Found

Since 2004, DHS's use of its CBRN risk assessments to inform its CBRN response plans has varied, from directly influencing information in the plans to not being used at all. DHS guidance states that response planning and resource decisions should be informed by risk information. GAO's analysis showed that DHS used its CBRN risk assessments to directly inform 2 of 12 CBRN response plans GAO identified because planners considered the risk assessments to be more accurate than earlier DHS planning assumptions. For another 7 of the 12 plans, DHS officials said that the assessments indirectly informed the plans by providing background information prior to plan development. However, GAO could not independently verify this because DHS officials could not document how the risk assessments influenced the information contained in the plans. GAO's analysis found general consistency between the risk assessments and the plans. For the remaining 3 plans, DHS officials did not use the risk assessments to inform the plans; for 2 of the 3 plans DHS officials told GAO they were not aware of the assessments. DHS officials also noted that there was no departmental guidance on when or how the CBRN risk assessments should be used when developing such plans.

Since 2004, DHS's use of its CBRN risk assessments to inform its CBRN-specific capabilities has varied, from directly impacting its capabilities to not being used at all. Of the 7 capabilities GAO reviewed, one was directly informed by the risk assessments; DHS used its biological agent risk assessments to confirm that its BioWatch program could generally detect the biological agents posing the greatest risk. For 5 of the 7 capabilities, DHS officials said they used the risk assessments along with other information sources to partially inform these capabilities. For example, DHS used its chemical agent risk assessments to determine whether its chemical detectors and the risk assessments were generally aligned for the highest risk agents. For 3 of these 5 capabilities, GAO could not independently verify that they were partially informed by the risk assessments because DHS officials could not document how the risk assessments influenced the capabilities. DHS did not use its CBRN risk assessments to inform the remaining CBRN capability because the assessments were not needed to meet the capability's mission.

DHS and its components do not have written procedures to institutionalize their use of DHS's CBRN risk assessments for CBRN response planning and capability investment decisions. Standards for internal control in the federal government call for written procedures to better ensure management's directives are enforced. DHS does not have procedures that stipulate when and how DHS officials should use the department's CBRN risk assessments to inform CBRN response planning and capability investment decisions, and GAO found variation in the extent to which they were used. DHS officials agree with GAO that without written procedures, the consistent use of the department's CBRN risk assessments by DHS officials may not be ensured beyond the tenure of any given agency official. DHS could better help to ensure that its CBRN response plans and capabilities are consistently informed by the department's CBRN risk assessments by establishing written procedures detailing when and how DHS officials should consider using the risk assessments to inform their activities.

_____ **United States Government Accountability Office**

Contents

Abbreviations

BTRA	Biological Terrorism Risk Assessment
CBRN	Chemical, biological, radiological, and nuclear
CFO's PAE	DHS Office of the Chief Financial Officer's Program Analysis and Evaluations unit
CONPLAN	Concept of Operations Plan
CTRA	Chemical Terrorism Risk Assessment
CSAC	Chemical Security Analysis Center
DHS	Department of Homeland Security
DNDO	Domestic Nuclear Detection Office

Executive Order 13527	Executive Order 13527 – Establishing Federal Capability for the Timely Provision of Medical Countermeasures Following a Biological Attack
FEMA	Federal Emergency Management Agency
FOUO	For Official Use Only
HHS	Department of Health and Human Services
HSPD 8 Annex I	Homeland Security Presidential Directive 8 – National Preparedness, Annex I – National Planning
IND	Improvised Nuclear Device
IPS	Integrated Planning System
ITRA	Integrated CBRN Terrorism Risk Assessment
MTA	Material Threat Assessment
NBFAC	National Bioforensic Analysis Center
NBIC	National Biosurveillance Integration Center
NPG	National Preparedness Guidelines
NIRT	Nuclear Incident Response Teams
NPPD's RMA	DHS National Protection and Programs Directorate's Office of Risk Management and Analysis
NPS	National Planning Scenario
NRF	National Response Framework
NRP	National Response Plan
NTNFC	National Technical Nuclear Forensics Center
OHA	DHS Office of Health Affairs
OPLAN	Operational Plan
OPS	DHS Office of Operations Coordination
PPD 8	Presidential Policy Directive 8 – National Preparedness
POLICY	DHS Office of Policy
RDCDS	Rapidly Deployable Chemical Detection System
RDD	Radiological Dispersal Device
R/NTRA	Radiological and Nuclear Terrorism Risk Assessment
S&T	DHS Science and Technology Directorate
SGS	Strategic Guidance Statement
STRATPLAN	Strategic Plan
TRA	Terrorism Risk Assessment

United States Government Accountability Office
Washington, DC 20548

January 25, 2012

The Honorable Joseph I. Lieberman
Chairman
The Honorable Susan M. Collins
Ranking Member
Committee on Homeland Security and Governmental Affairs
United States Senate

The anthrax attacks of 2001 raised concerns that the United States is vulnerable to threats from chemical, biological, radiological, and nuclear (CBRN) agents. Moreover, the 2007 *National Strategy for Homeland Security* stated that terrorists have declared their intention to acquire and use CBRN agents as weapons to inflict catastrophic attacks against the United States.[1] More recently, the May 2010 *National Security Strategy* noted that the American people face no greater or more urgent danger than a terrorist attack with a nuclear weapon. The strategy further said that the effective dissemination of a lethal biological agent within a U.S. city would endanger the lives of hundreds of thousands of people and have unprecedented economic, societal, and political consequences.[2] In addition, multiple stakeholders have assessed the federal government's ability to protect the nation from CBRN agents and deemed it inadequate. For example, in January 2010, the congressionally mandated Commission on the Prevention of Weapons of Mass Destruction Proliferation and Terrorism reported that the federal government lacked the capability to rapidly recognize, respond to, and recover from a terrorist attack using biological agents.

Because CBRN agents differ in their potential to be used to cause widespread illness and death, members of Congress have expressed the need for the Department of Homeland Security (DHS) to assess the risks posed by CBRN agents to identify those that are highest risk and develop

---

[1]White House – Homeland Security Council, *National Strategy for Homeland Security* (Washington, D.C.: October 2007).

[2]White House, *National Security Strategy* (Washington, D.C.: May 2010).

necessary response plans and capabilities.[3] To address these needs, DHS produces CBRN threat and risk assessments that analyze the potential for adverse outcomes as a result of an attack with such agents. Since 2004, DHS has spent over $70 million developing these analyses. Assessing the risks posed by CBRN agents requires analyzing and modeling areas of uncertainty, including determining an adversary's capability to acquire these agents, develop them into weapons, and disseminate them to estimate the plausibility and consequences of such attacks. These assessments are designed so that decision makers can use them to inform priorities, develop or compare courses of action, and inform federal planning and investments for responding to the highest risk CBRN incidents.

The 2007 National Strategy for Homeland Security (Strategy) notes that the nation must apply a risk-based framework across all homeland security efforts to identify and assess potential hazards, determine what levels of relative risk are acceptable, and prioritize and allocate resources among homeland security partners to, among other things, respond to and recover from CBRN incidents. The Strategy states that a disciplined approach to managing risk will help to achieve overall effectiveness and efficiency in securing the nation. Further, the Strategy notes that for homeland security efforts to succeed federal dollars must be allocated based on risk assessments and on accountability for results; once allocated, funds must be used to support or develop operational plans and their derivative requirements and capabilities.

In June 2011 we reported on DHS and the Department of Health and Human Services (HHS) coordination for developing CBRN risk assessments.[4] We found that DHS and HHS have coordinated with each other and with other federal departments to varying extents over time to develop CBRN risk assessments, but that neither department has written procedures for developing these assessments. We recommended that

---

[3]For the purposes of this report, response plans refer to strategic, conceptual, and operational CBRN scenario-specific plans and related annexes developed to define interagency roles, responsibilities, and tasks for responding to a CBRN incident. Capabilities provide the means to respond to CBRN incidents through organization, equipment, training, exercises, and personnel.

[4]GAO, *National Preparedness: DHS and HHS Can Further Strengthen Coordination for Chemical, Biological, Radiological, and Nuclear Risk Assessments*, GAO-11-606 (Washington, D.C.: June 2011).

DHS develop time frames and milestones to better ensure timely development of and interagency agreement on written procedures for the development of its CBRN risk assessments, and DHS agreed with our recommendation. DHS stated that the department had begun efforts to develop milestones and time frames for development of strategic and implementation plans for interagency CBRN risk assessment development.

You asked us to examine DHS's use of its CBRN risk assessments. This report assesses the extent to which, from 2004 to the present, DHS (1) used its CBRN risk assessments to inform its CBRN response plans and (2) CBRN capabilities, and (3) institutionalized the use of its CBRN risk assessments for such activities through written policies and procedures.

This report is a public version of the prior classified report that we provided to you. DHS deemed some of the information in the prior report as sensitive or classified, which must be protected from public disclosure. Therefore, this report omits sensitive or classified information contained in DHS's CBRN risk assessments and CBRN response plans. In addition, this report omits sensitive or classified information about DHS CBRN capabilities. Although the information provided in this report is more limited in scope, it addresses the same objectives as the classified report. Also, the overall methodology used for both reports is the same.

To address objectives 1 and 2, we analyzed relevant federal laws, presidential directives, executive orders, and national strategies. For example, we reviewed presidential directives on national preparedness and CBRN-related activities and an executive order on the distribution of medical countermeasures in the event of a domestic biological attack. We analyzed these documents to identify requirements for DHS to develop CBRN risk assessments as well as interagency CBRN-specific response plans and capabilities, and for any criteria contained within these documents to guide the use of DHS's CBRN risk assessments to inform response planning activities and capability program management. We analyzed the CBRN risk assessments, response plans, and documents on the capabilities DHS has developed since 2004—the year initial legislative requirements were enacted for the department to develop the assessments—to determine the contents of these assessments and these plans. For the purposes of this report, we consider DHS's CBRN risk assessments to include its Terrorism Risk Assessments (TRAs) and Material Threat Assessments (MTAs).[5]

We analyzed all 12 CBRN-specific interagency response plans developed by DHS that are designed for responding to CBRN incidents to determine the extent to which they identify DHS's CBRN risk assessments as a source of information contained within the plans.[6] We also asked DHS officials to provide us with documentation showing how specific information from the risk assessments, if any, was incorporated into the plans. We then reviewed the response plans to identify CBRN agent-specific planning assumptions contained within the plans. We selected assumptions that contained information about the unique features of the CBRN agent, the threat, the attack scenario, DHS's ability to detect the agent and respond, public health consequences of an attack, or time frames for response. We excluded generic statements regarding coordination of the federal response to an attack and the roles and responsibilities of relevant agencies because the CBRN risk assessments do not assess these topics. We compared these assumptions to the information contained in the risk assessments to determine the relative level of consistency between examples of this type of information contained in the plans and in the assessments.[7] Our analysis did not

---

[5]DHS also develops other non-CBRN-specific risk assessments which we did not review. TRAs assess the risks posed by CBRN agents based on variable threats, vulnerabilities, and consequences. MTAs assess the threat posed by given CBRN agents and the potential number of human exposures in plausible high-consequence scenarios. According to the *DHS Risk Lexicon*, threats are entities, actions, or occurrences, whether natural or man-made, that have or indicate the potential to harm life, information, operations, and/or property; vulnerabilities are physical features or operational attributes that render an entity, asset, system, network, or geographic area susceptible or exposed to hazards; and consequences are potential or actual effects of an event, incident, or occurrence. DHS, *DHS Risk Lexicon: 2010 Edition* (Washington, D.C.: September 2010).

[6]For the purposes of this report, we included all interagency response plans developed by DHS for responding to CBRN-specific incidents. We did not include internally developed DHS intraagency plans for CBRN events and interagency response plans that could be used to respond to CBRN incidents but that are designed for responding to all-hazards.

[7]For the purposes of this report, we define planning assumptions within the CBRN response plans as the information contained in the plans related to CBRN-specific threats, vulnerabilities, and consequences. Planning assumptions form the foundational basis upon which a response plan is developed. This understanding is necessary to enable leaders and planners to develop potential courses of action to address a given CBRN incident.

compare all assumptions in the plans, including those that were non-CBRN agent specific, to all the assumptions in the risk assessments.

Further, we identified a nongeneralizable set of seven CBRN-specific capabilities by interviewing DHS component program officials and conducting a search of a Department of Defense database that contains a listing of U.S. governmentwide CBRN capabilities and activities. We used these interviews and the database to limit our scope to capabilities that are specifically deployed and are being used by DHS components to prevent, detect, and respond to CBRN incidents. We did not include within our scope capabilities for responding to all-hazards that may also be used for responding to CBRN incidents, nor did we include, among others, capabilities related to intelligence, law enforcement, training, or research and development. We reviewed documentation of these programs to determine the extent to which they are informed by DHS's CBRN risk assessments. When possible, we directly compared the lists of threat agents that are addressed by the capabilities to the relevant lists of high-risk agents identified in the CBRN risk assessments. We did not compare any other information in the CBRN risk assessments—such as assumptions about U.S. vulnerabilities to specific threat agents or attack consequences—to the capabilities.

We also interviewed officials from DHS offices, components, and agencies to obtain information on whether and how they used the TRAs and MTAs in developing a given response plan or developing and managing a given capability. Specifically, we interviewed DHS officials from DHS's:

- Science and Technology Directorate (S&T),
- Office of the Chief Financial Officer (CFO), Program Analysis and Evaluations (PA&E),
- Office of Health Affairs (OHA),
- Office of Operations Coordination (OPS),
- Office of Policy (POLICY),
- National Protection and Programs Directorate's (NPPD) Office of Risk Management and Analysis (RMA),
- Domestic Nuclear Detection Office (DNDO), and
- Federal Emergency Management Agency (FEMA).

To address the third objective, we analyzed *Standards for Internal Control in the Federal Government* for guidelines on internal controls.[8] We then obtained written policies or procedures developed by DHS offices, components, or agencies that describe whether and how DHS's CBRN risk assessments should be used when DHS officials develop CBRN response plans or capabilities. We compared the standards for internal control against the status of DHS's development of policies and procedures for using its CBRN risk assessments to inform its plans and capabilities. We also interviewed DHS officials to obtain information on the reasons why DHS has or has not institutionalized use of the TRAs and MTAs through written policies and procedures.

We conducted this performance audit from February through December 2011 in accordance with generally accepted government auditing standards. Those standards require that we plan and perform the audit to obtain sufficient, appropriate evidence to provide a reasonable basis for our findings and conclusions based on our audit objectives. We believe that the evidence obtained provides a reasonable basis for our findings and conclusions based on our audit objectives.

Background

Multiple DHS offices, components, and agencies have roles and responsibilities in DHS's development of CBRN risk assessments, response plans, and capabilities. Specifically:

- S&T is responsible for the development of DHS's CBRN risk assessments—the TRAs and MTAs.

- CFO's PA&E unit is responsible for developing resource allocation decisions for capability investments through DHS's Planning, Programming, Budgeting and Execution system.

---

[8]GAO, *Standards for Internal Control in the Federal Government*, GAO/AIMD-00-21.3.1 (Washington, D.C.: November 1999). The criteria in GAO/AIMD 00-21.3.1, dated November 1999, issued pursuant to the requirements of the Federal Managers' Financial Integrity Act of 1982 (FMFIA), provide the overall framework for establishing and maintaining internal control in the federal government. Also pursuant to FMFIA, the Office of Management and Budget issued Circular A-123, revised December 21, 2004, to provide the specific requirements for assessing the reporting on internal controls. Internal control standards and the definition of internal control in Circular A-123 are based on GAO's *Standards for Internal Control in the Federal Government*. See also the Related GAO Products section at the end of this report.

- OHA is responsible for leading DHS's biological and chemical defense activities and provides medical and public health expertise to support the department's efforts.

- OPS is responsible for coordinating DHS's operational activities for incident response, including for CBRN incidents.

- POLICY is responsible for advising the Secretary of Homeland Security in the development of DHS's policies for CBRN plans and capabilities.

- NPPD's RMA is responsible for leading DHS's approach to risk management and the application of risk information to departmental activities.

- DNDO is responsible for domestic radiological and nuclear detection efforts and integration of federal nuclear forensics programs.

- FEMA is responsible for leading the nation's effort for preparing to respond to emergencies and disasters.

DHS Risk Management

DHS engages in risk management activities to help ensure the nation's ability to protect against and respond to incidents using CBRN agents.[9] DHS's Risk Lexicon provides the following definitions for risk-related terms:[10]

- Risk—potential for an adverse outcome assessed as a function of threats, vulnerabilities, and consequences associated with an incident, event, or occurrence.

- Risk Assessment—product or process which collects information and assigns values to risks for the purpose of informing priorities, developing or comparing courses of action, and informing decision making.

- Risk Management—process of identifying, analyzing, assessing, and communicating risk and accepting, avoiding, transferring, or

---

[9]DHS, *Quadrennial Homeland Security Review* (Washington, D.C.: February 2010).

[10]DHS, *DHS Risk Lexicon: 2010 Edition* (Washington, D.C.: September 2010).

controlling it to an acceptable level considering associated costs and benefits of any actions taken.

The department's 2010 *Quadrennial Homeland Security Review* notes the importance of incorporating information from risk assessments into departmental decision making, one aspect of the department's homeland security risk management process.[11] According to DHS doctrine, risk management applications include the use of risk information to inform, among others, strategic and operational planning and resource decisions. This report focuses on DHS's use of the third step of its risk management process—risk assessment—and the application of risk assessment results to inform CBRN response plans and capabilities. DHS notes that risk information is usually one of many factors—not necessarily the sole factor—that decision makers consider when deciding which strategies to pursue for managing risk. These additional factors may include strategic and political considerations, among others. See figure 1 for a graphic depiction of DHS's risk management process.

---

[11]DHS has standardized its risk management process to include the following steps: (1) defining and framing the context of decisions and related goals and objectives; (2) identifying the risks associated with the goals and objectives; (3) analyzing and assessing the identified risks (i.e., risk assessment); (4) developing alternative actions for managing the risks and creating opportunities, and analyzing the costs and benefits of those alternatives; (5) making a decision among alternatives and implementing that decision; and (6) monitoring the implemented decision and comparing observed and expected effects to help influence subsequent risk management alternatives and decisions. This process was codified in the DHS Interim Integrated Risk Management Framework of January 2009, and reissued in the doctrinal document DHS Risk Management Fundamentals in April 2011. DHS, *Interim Integrated Risk Management Framework* (Washington, D.C.: January 2009) and DHS, *Risk Management Fundamentals: Homeland Security Risk Management Doctrine* (Washington, D.C.: April 2011).

Figure 1: DHS's Risk Management Process

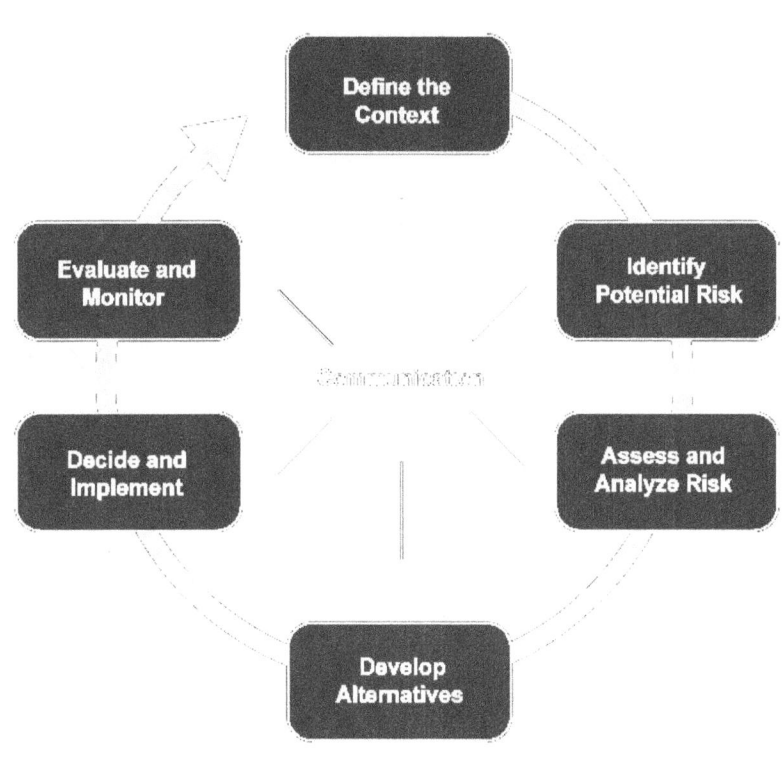

Source: DHS Risk Management Fundamentals.

DHS's CBRN Risk Assessments

DHS is responsible for assessing the risks posed by various CBRN agents, as directed by the Project BioShield Act of 2004[12] and Homeland Security Presidential Directives 10 – Biodefense for the 21st Century, 18 – *Medical Countermeasures against Weapons of Mass Destruction*, and 22 – *National Domestic Chemical Defense*. To this end, S&T develops CBRN TRAs and MTAs.[13]

---

[12]42 U.S.C. § 247d-6b(c)(2)(A).

[13]For more details on DHS's TRAs and MTAs, see GAO-11-606.

Each TRA assesses the relative risks posed by multiple CBRN agents based on variable threats, vulnerabilities, and consequences. Since 2006, DHS has developed eight TRA reports:

- Biological Terrorism Risk Assessments (BTRA) in 2006, 2008, and 2010;
- Chemical Terrorism Risk Assessments (CTRA) in 2008 and 2010;
- Radiological/Nuclear Terrorism Risk Assessment (R/NTRA) in 2011; and
- Integrated CBRN Terrorism Risk Assessments (ITRA) in 2008 and 2011.

Each MTA assesses the threat posed by a given, individual CBRN agent or class of agents and the potential number of human exposures in plausible, high-consequence scenarios. Since 2004, DHS has developed 17 MTA reports. DHS uses the MTAs to determine which CBRN agents pose a material threat sufficient to affect national security.[14]

The Project BioShield Act describes specific ways in which the MTAs may be used in efforts to procure certain medical countermeasures.[15] However, the various presidential directives note that while the TRAs may be used to inform decision making, they are not specific as to when or how these risk assessments should be used by DHS officials to inform CBRN response planning or capability investments.

DHS's CBRN Response Plans and Capabilities

(U) We identified CBRN-specific interagency response plans among three families of interagency plans developed by DHS that are designed for responding to CBRN incidents. These families of plans include plans developed under (1) Executive Order 13527 – Establishing Federal Capability for the Timely Provision of Medical Countermeasures Following a Biological Attack (Executive Order 13527) and (2) Homeland Security Presidential Directive 8 Annex I – National Planning (HSPD 8 Annex I), and as a part of (3) the National Response Framework's (NRF) CBRN-

---

[14]Since 2004, DHS determined that 14 of 17 CBRN agents that it assessed in MTAs pose a material threat to the nation and issued material threat determinations for those agents. For more details on DHS's material threat determinations, see GAO-11-606.

[15]See 42 U.S.C. § 247d-6b(c).

specific incident annexes.[16,17] See table 1 for a listing of the 12 plans we reviewed.

Table 1: DHS's CBRN-specific Interagency Response Plans Reviewed

Response plan family	CBRN-specific response plan[a]
Executive Order 13527 – Establishing Federal Capability for the Timely Provision of Medical Countermeasures Following a Biological Attack (related plans issued in 2010)	
In response to requirements in Executive Order 13527, DHS developed three plans in coordination with its interagency partners that are designed to reduce the potential for large numbers of casualties and fatalities in the United States following a geographically dispersed biological attack. These plans were developed to address a range of activities necessary for responding to such incidents.	U.S. Postal Service Medical Countermeasure Dispensing Model and Annex on Law Enforcement Support to the Postal Model
	Operational Concepts and Requirements for a Federal Medical Countermeasures Rapid Response and related Federal Interagency Operational Plan: Rapid Medical Countermeasure Dispensing
	Plan for the Provision of Medical Countermeasures to Ensure Continuity of Federal Mission Essential Functions
Homeland Security Presidential Directive 8 Annex I – National Planning (related plans issued 2008-2009)	
HSPD-8 Annex I called for the development of a standardized federal planning process—the Integrated Planning System (IPS)—and a family of response plans using IPS and the National Planning Scenarios (NPS), including strategic guidance statements (SGS), strategic plans (STRATPLANS), concepts of operation plans (CONPLANS), and operations plans (OPLANS).[b] One SGS and three STRATPLANS (with related annexes) were developed under IPS for the CBRN-specific NPS prior to this effort being put on an indefinite hold in July 2009 by the White House National Security Staff pending the revision of HSPD 8.[c] Presidential Policy Directive 8 – *National Preparedness* (PPD 8) superseded HSPD 8 Annex I and its provisions on March 30, 2011.[d]	SGS for Chemical Attacks
	STRATPLAN for Biological Attacks[e] • Annex A: Aerosol Anthrax • Annex B: Plague • Annex C: Food Contamination • Annex D: Foot and Mouth Disease
	STRATPLAN for Terrorist Use of Radiological Dispersal Devices
	STRATPLAN for Terrorist Use of an Improvised Nuclear Device

[16]Exec. Order No. 13,527, 75 *Fed. Reg.* 737 (Dec. 30, 2009); and White House, Homeland Security Presidential Directive 8 *(National Preparedness)* Annex I – *National Planning* (Washington, D.C.: December 2007). HSPD 8 and its Annex I were superseded by Presidential Policy Directive 8 – *National Preparedness* on March 30, 2011.

[17]DHS, *National Response Framework* (Washington, D.C.: January 2008). For the purposes of this report, we considered CBRN-specific incident annexes in the NRF to be CBRN response plans. DHS issued the National Response Plan (NRP) in December 2004 and made some revisions to the plan in May 2006 to address lessons learned from Hurricane Katrina. The National Response Framework (NRF) was issued as a full revision and replacement of the NRP in January 2008.

Response plan family	CBRN-specific response plan[a]
National Response Framework (related annexes originally issued in 2004 and reissued in 2008)	
Developed by FEMA and issued by DHS, the NRF is the doctrine that guides how federal, state, local, and tribal governments, along with nongovernmental and private sector entities, will collectively respond to and recover from all-hazards including CBRN incidents. The NRF includes, among others, seven Incident Annexes which are to address aspects of how the United States responds to specific types of incidents. Two of these incident annexes are for CBRN events.	Biological Incident Annex
	Nuclear/Radiological Incident Annex

Source: GAO analysis of presidential and DHS documents.

[a]For the purposes of this report, in addition to stand-alone plans, we also refer to CBRN-specific annexes as "plans."

[b]DHS, National Planning Scenarios (Washington, D.C.: April 2005). The NPS establish common assumptions regarding potential vulnerabilities and consequences posed by plausible, high-consequence natural disasters and terrorist incidents, including attacks with CBRN agents, to guide emergency response planning nationwide.

[c]For the purposes of this report, we reviewed the most detailed response plan developed under HSPD 8 Annex I for a given CBRN agent. Specifically, if an SGS was developed but a related STRATPLAN had not been, we analyzed the SGS for the given agent. If a STRATPLAN had been developed, but a related CONPLAN had not been, we analyzed the STRATPLAN for the given agent. Although a CONPLAN for responding to an improvised nuclear device (IND) was issued by DHS in an interim format in November 2009, we only reviewed the IND STRATPLAN because it was the most detailed finalized plan produced.

[d]PPD 8 states that plans developed under HSPD 8 Annex I remain in effect until rescinded. The implementation plan for PPD 8, issued in May 2011, directs DHS to develop national planning frameworks for the prevention, protection, mitigation, response, and recovery mission areas by June 30, 2012, and related interagency operational plans for each of these frameworks by September 25, 2012. The implementation plan notes that the frameworks are intended to align key roles and responsibilities for the delivery of necessary capabilities for each mission area. The implementation plan also notes that the related interagency operational plans for each mission area are to support the various frameworks and describe the concept of operations for integrating and synchronizing existing national level capabilities to support federal, state, local, tribal, and territorial plans.

[e]For the purposes of this report we consider the STRATPLAN for Biological Attacks to count as four plans because it contains four agent- or incident-specific annexes. We reviewed each annex as if it were a stand-alone plan.

Presidential Policy Directive 8 – National Preparedness, issued in March 2011, superseded HSPD 8 Annex I and its requirement for SGS, STRATPLANs, CONPLANs, and OPLANS to be developed for each NPS.[18] In May 2011 DHS issued an implementation plan for the new directive which calls for DHS to develop an interagency operational plan to implement the NRF by September 2012. According to FEMA officials, this interagency operational plan may include a range of incident

---

[18]One SGS, three STRATPLANS, and four related STRATPLAN annexes were developed under IPS for the CBRN-specific NPS prior to these planning efforts being put on an indefinite hold in July 2009 by the White House National Security Staff pending the revision of HSPD 8. Presidential Policy Directive 8 replaced HSPD 8 in March 2011.

annexes, potentially including annexes specific to CBRN incidents. This operational plan and related annexes have yet to be developed.

We selected seven CBRN-specific capabilities managed by DHS that are designed to prevent, detect, or respond to CBRN incidents to assess the extent to which these capabilities are informed by DHS's CBRN risk assessments. These seven capabilities are managed by various DHS components, including OHA, S&T, FEMA, and DNDO. Table 2 provides a listing of the DHS CBRN capabilities we analyzed and a description of each program.

Table 2: Select DHS CBRN-specific Capabilities Reviewed

Capability and DHS component	Description of capability
Select chemical capabilities	
Rapidly Deployable Chemical Detection System (RDCDS) *OHA*	The RDCDS is a mobile set of chemical detectors that can be deployed across the nation and set up prior to large public events. The RDCDS detectors can be programmed to detect specific chemical threat agents and in the event of an attack, the detectors are intended to enable federal, state, and local officials to quickly identify the agent and respond.
Chemical Security Analysis Center (CSAC) *S&T*	The CSAC works to provide a scientific basis for understanding the risks posed by chemical threat agents and for attribution associated with their use in a terrorist attack. The CSAC is a resource that provides a centralized compilation of chemical hazard data, using these data to assess chemical threats through risk assessments and other products.
Select biological capabilities	
BioWatch *OHA*	BioWatch is a federally managed, locally operated biosurveillance system of air sample collectors designed to detect the release of select aerosolized bioterrorism agents. In the event of such a release, BioWatch is intended to enable federal, state, and local officials to identify the agent and respond.
National Bioforensic Analysis Center (NBFAC) *S&T*	The NBFAC conducts bioforensic analysis of evidence from a biocrime or terrorist attack to attain a "biological fingerprint" to help investigators identify perpetrators and determine the origin and method of attack. The NBFAC is designated by Homeland Security Presidential Directive 10 – *Biodefense for the 21st Century* to be the lead federal facility to conduct and facilitate the technical forensic analysis and interpretation of materials recovered following a biological attack in support of the appropriate lead federal agency.
National Biosurveillance Integration Center *OHA*	The NBIC works to integrate and analyze information from biosurveillance systems across the federal government, and to disseminate alerts if any biological events are detected.

Capability and DHS component	Description of capability
Select radiological and nuclear capabilities	
Nuclear Incident Response Teams (NIRT) *FEMA*	The NIRTs are specialized teams managed day to day by the Department of Energy's National Nuclear Security Administration and the Environmental Protection Agency. In the event of a high-consequence nuclear incident, the NIRTs fall under FEMA's operational control. FEMA works to provide expert technical advice and support in disaster response operations and other needs involving nuclear weapons accidents, radiological accidents, lost or stolen nuclear material incidents, and acts of nuclear terrorism.
National Technical Nuclear Forensics Center (NTNFC) *DNDO*	The NTNFC has two primary missions. The first is to provide centralized planning, integration, and stewardship of the nation's nuclear forensics activities to ensure a ready, robust, and enduring capability in coordination with other federal departments and agencies. The second is to advance technical capabilities in the area of predetonation forensics for radiological and nuclear materials.

Source: GAO analysis of DHS documents and information provided by DHS officials.

DHS Used Its CBRN Risk Assessments to Directly or Indirectly Inform 9 of 12 of Its CBRN Response Plans

Since the first DHS CBRN risk assessments were developed in 2004, DHS used the risk assessments to varying degrees to directly or indirectly inform development of 9 of the 12 CBRN-specific response plans we identified.[19] Our analysis showed that 2 of the 12 plans were directly informed by the risk assessments, while DHS officials told us that 7 of the 12 plans were indirectly informed by the risk assessments. However, we could not independently verify this for these 7 plans because DHS officials could not document how the risk assessments influenced information contained in the plans. Three of the response plans were not informed by the risk assessments, according to DHS officials. Our analysis of a limited set of planning assumptions in the plans compared to information contained in the risk assessments showed general consistency between the plans and the risk assessments.

DHS's guidelines state that response plans should be informed by risk assessment information to supplement risk-related information contained in the National Planning Scenarios (NPS) used for developing emergency

---

[19]For the purposes of this report, we refer to CBRN response plans as being directly informed by DHS's CBRN risk assessments if the plans specifically identify the TRAs or MTAs as a source for information contained within the plan, or if DHS officials were able to provide documentation showing how specific information from the risk assessments was incorporated into the plan. We refer to CBRN response plans as being indirectly informed by DHS's CBRN risk assessments if DHS officials said that the TRAs or MTAs served as a source of background information that was known to officials involved in the development of the plans, but the plans do not specifically identify the risk assessments as a source for information contained in the plans and DHS officials were unable to provide documentation showing their use.

response plans.[20,21] DHS's 2009 Integrated Planning System (IPS) also identifies risk assessments as one source of information that should be used to inform response plan development.[22] This guidance, however, does not define what it means for response plans to be informed by risk assessments or how planners should use specific types of risk assessments, such as DHS's TRAs and MTAs, when developing or revising related plans. Of the 12 CBRN response plans developed by DHS that we reviewed, none of the plans were developed solely in response to a given CBRN threat agent being identified as high risk in DHS's CBRN risk assessments. Rather, these plans were developed in response to requirements in an executive order and as part of families of plans developed in response to provisions in presidential directives.[23] See table 3 for a list of the CBRN response plans and whether each plan was directly, indirectly, or not informed by DHS's CBRN risk assessments during its development.

---

[20]DHS, *Interim National Preparedness Goal* (Washington, D.C.: March 2005) and DHS, *National Preparedness Guidelines* (Washington, D.C.: September 2007). The National Preparedness Guidelines replaced the Interim National Preparedness Goal in 2007. Both were developed to define what it means for the nation to be prepared for responding to emergencies arising from man-made or natural disasters.

[21]DHS, *National Planning Scenarios* (Washington, D.C.: April 2005). According to the National Preparedness Guidelines, the 15 National Planning Scenarios establish common assumptions regarding potential vulnerabilities and consequences posed by plausible, high-consequence natural disasters and terrorist incidents, including attacks with CBRN agents, to guide emergency response planning nationwide.

[22]White House, *Integrated Planning System* (Washington, D.C.: January 2009). The Integrated Planning System was developed to establish a standardized approach to national planning, in response to requirements in Homeland Security Presidential Directive 8 Annex I – *National Planning*.

[23]Exec. Order No. 13,527, 75 *Fed. Reg.* 737 (Dec. 30, 2009); White House, Homeland Security Presidential Directive 5 – Management of Domestic Incidents (Washington, D.C.: February 2003); and White House, Homeland Security Presidential Directive 8 – *National Preparedness,* Annex I – *National Planning* (Washington, D.C.: December 2007). In response to a requirement contained in Homeland Security Presidential Directive 5, DHS issued the National Response Plan (NRP) in December 2004 and made some revisions to the plan in May 2006 to address lessons learned from Hurricane Katrina. The National Response Framework (NRF) replaced the NRP in January 2008. HSPD 8 and its Annex I were superseded by Presidential Policy Directive 8 – *National Preparedness* on March 30, 2011.

Table 3: Extent to Which DHS's CBRN Risk Assessments Informed Development of its CBRN Response Plans

Response plan-family	CBRN response plan[a]	Informed by DHS's CBRN risk assessments[c]
Executive Order 13527 – Establishing Federal Capability for the Timely Provision of Medical Countermeasures Following a Biological Attack (related plans issued in 2010)	U.S. Postal Service Medical Countermeasure Dispensing Model and Annex on Law Enforcement Support to the Postal Model	Indirectly
	Operational Concepts and Requirements for a Federal Medical Countermeasures Rapid Response and related Federal Interagency Operational Plan: Rapid Medical Countermeasure Dispensing	Indirectly
	Plan for the Provision of Medical Countermeasures to Ensure Continuity of Federal Mission Essential Functions	Indirectly
Homeland Security Presidential Directive 8 Annex I – National Planning (related plans issued 2008-2009)	SGS for Chemical Attacks	Indirectly
	STRATPLAN for Biological Attacks[b]	
	• Annex A: Aerosol Anthrax	Directly
	• Annex B: Plague	Directly
	• Annex C: Food Contamination	Indirectly
	• Annex D: Foot and Mouth Disease	No
	STRATPLAN for Terrorist Use of Radiological Dispersal Devices	Indirectly
	STRATPLAN for Terrorist Use of an Improvised Nuclear Device	Indirectly
National Response Framework (related annexes originally issued in 2004 and reissued in 2008)	Biological Incident Annex	No
	Nuclear/Radiological Incident Annex	No

Source: GAO analysis of presidential and DHS documents and information provided by DHS officials.

[a]For the purposes of this report, in addition to stand-alone plans, we refer to CBRN-specific annexes as "plans."

[b]For the purposes of this report we consider the STRATPLAN for Biological Attacks to count as four plans because it contains four agent- or incident-specific annexes. We reviewed each annex as if it were a stand-alone plan.

[c]For the purposes of this report, we identify a response plan as being directly informed by DHS's CBRN risk assessments if the plan specifically identifies the TRAs or MTAs as a source for information contained within the plan, or if DHS officials were able to provide documentation showing how specific information from the risk assessments was incorporated into the plan. We identify a response plan as being indirectly informed by DHS's CBRN risk assessments if DHS officials said that the TRAs or MTAs served as a source of background information that was known to officials involved in the development of the plans, but the plans do not specifically identify the risk assessments as a source for information contained in the plans and DHS officials were unable to provide documentation showing their use.

All Three Biological Response Plans Developed under Executive Order 13527 Were Indirectly Informed by DHS's CBRN Risk assessments

The three biological response plans developed in response to Executive Order 13527 were indirectly informed by DHS's CBRN risk assessments, according to DHS officials, but officials could not provide documentation showing how the risk assessments influenced the development of these plans. The plans developed under this order are designed to implement the administration's policy of preparing for the timely provision of medical countermeasures to the American people in the event of a biological attack—in particular an aerosolized anthrax attack—to mitigate potential illnesses and deaths.

According to officials from OHA—which led development of all three plans for DHS—both the BTRA and anthrax MTA were used to help educate planners prior to the development of the plans.[24] The BTRA and anthrax MTA were used, according to OHA officials, because they provided planners with scientifically-based information on the threat, vulnerabilities, and consequences posed by an aerosolized anthrax attack. OHA officials said that this helped inform initial discussions in the interagency workgroups that were responsible for developing the plans.

OHA planners stated that the BTRA served as a source of background information on the risk posed by anthrax relative to other biological agents. The planners also said they used the 2005 anthrax MTA and a 2008 unclassified version of the anthrax MTA to help understand the specific planning assumptions that would need to be addressed by the three plans.[25] OHA officials said they used these MTAs because the anthrax MTAs provide more up-to-date and accurate information on the exposures and potential casualties that would occur during an anthrax attack than is provided in the 2005 anthrax NPS. As a result, according to DHS officials, these plans were better informed than they would have been had the anthrax NPS been the sole source of background information used to develop the plans.

---

[24]In addition to DHS, departments and agencies involved in the development of the plans under Executive Order 13527 included, among others, the Department of Health and Human Services, Department of Defense, Department of Justice, and the U.S. Postal Service.

[25]The classified anthrax MTA was published in April 2005. A for-official-use-only (FOUO) version of this MTA was published in March 2008 at the request of OHA. The FOUO version is based on the classified version of the document, but also incorporates, among other things, additional information on the health effects of such an attack as determined by officials from HHS.

DHS officials could not produce documentation showing how the BTRA and the anthrax MTAs influenced the development of these plans. As a result, we could not independently verify that the risk assessments were used by DHS officials to influence development of the plans. Our analysis of a limited set of planning assumptions in the plans compared to information contained in the DHS CBRN risk assessments showed general consistency between the information contained in the plans and the information contained in the risk assessments.[26]

DHS officials emphasized that the DHS CBRN risk assessments are just one source of data among many that DHS planners used in the course of their planning activities under the executive order. According to officials, additional sources of information included, among others, current intelligence information, emerging scientific research on CBRN threat agents, and the subject matter expertise of officials from DHS, HHS, DOD, and others who were involved in the development of the plans.

Six of the Seven CBRN Response Plans Developed under HSPD-8 Annex I Were Directly or Indirectly Informed by DHS's CBRN Risk Assessments

Our analysis showed that two of the seven CBRN response plans developed under HSPD 8 Annex I—the anthrax and plague annexes—were directly informed by DHS's CBRN risk assessments. Four of the seven plans were indirectly informed by the risk assessments, according to DHS officials: the SGS for chemical attacks, STRATPLANs for radiological and nuclear device attacks, and the food contamination annex. However, officials could not provide documentation showing how the risk assessments influenced the development of these plans. As a result, we could not independently verify that the risk assessments were used by DHS officials to influence development of the plans. The last plan—the foot and mouth disease annex—was not informed by the risk assessments. The seven plans were created to address provisions in HSPD 8 Annex I that called for the establishment of a family of plans that were to be developed for each NPS to enhance national

---

[26]We omitted from this report examples from a limited set of Executive Order 13527 planning assumptions compared to CBRN risk assessment content because DHS deemed this information as sensitive or classified.

preparedness.[27,28] IPS, which was developed as directed by Annex I, was designed to establish a standardized approach to federal planning. IPS states that planners should use risk assessments as one source of information to inform the development of response plans.[29]

According to officials from OPS—which served as the lead for the interagency team that developed the plans—DHS's TRAs and MTAs were used to either directly or indirectly inform all but one of the plans. OPS officials noted that they were briefed on the contents of the TRAs to understand the relative risks posed by various CBRN threat agents in the course of collecting background information to inform their planning efforts. OPS officials also reviewed the MTAs during their background research, which they said were useful because they provided specific

---

[27]These seven plans were developed and finalized for the CBRN-specific NPS prior to planning under HSPD 8 Annex I being put on indefinite hold in July 2009 by the White House National Security Staff pending the revision of HSPD 8. Presidential Policy Directive 8 – National Preparedness (PPD 8) superseded HSPD 8 Annex I and its provisions on March 30, 2011. For the purposes of this report, we analyzed the most detailed finalized response plans developed under HSPD 8 Annex I for a given CBRN agent. PPD 8 states that plans developed under HSPD 8 Annex I remain in effect until rescinded.

[28]HSPD 8 Annex I directed the Secretary of Homeland Security to develop strategic guidance statements (SGS), strategic plans (STRATPLANS), concept of operations plans (CONPLANS), and operational plans (OPLANS) for each NPS. SGS were to be documents that outlined strategic priorities, broad national strategic objectives, and basic assumptions; described the envisioned end state; and established the general means necessary to accomplish that end for each NPS. STRATPLANS were to be based off of the related SGS for each NPS and were to be plans that defined the mission, identified authorities, delineated roles and responsibilities, established mission-essential tasks, determined required and priority capabilities, and developed performance and effectiveness measures. CONPLANS were to be based off of the related STRATPLAN for each NPS and were to be plans that briefly described the concept of operations for integrating and synchronizing existing federal capabilities to accomplish the mission-essential tasks, and described how federal capabilities were to be integrated into and support regional, state, local, and tribal plans for each NPS. OPLANS were to be based off of the related CONPLAN for each NPS and were to be developed by each federal department and agency. These OPLANS were to be plans that identified detailed resource, personnel, and asset allocations to execute the objectives of the strategic plan and turn strategic priorities into operational execution, and were to contain the full description of the concept of operations, to include specific roles and responsibilities, tasks, integration, and actions required, with supplemental support function annexes as appropriate.

[29]IPS states that planners employ risk assessment to support, organize, and prioritize planning activities using planning scenarios and that planners should update existing plans if risk levels change based on new or updated risk assessments.

planning assumptions for plausible, high-consequence attacks using such agents. Specifically, OPS used:

- the anthrax and plague MTAs to directly inform development of the anthrax and plague annexes issued in May 2009,[30]
- the 2008 CTRA and various chemical MTAs to indirectly inform development of the Chemical Attack SGS issued in June 2009,[31]
- the Nuclear/Radiological Appendix to the 2008 Integrated CBRN TRA (ITRA) and radiological and nuclear agent MTA to indirectly inform development of the Radiological Dispersal and Improvised Nuclear Device STRATPLANS, and
- the 2008 BTRA, CTRA, and ITRA, as well as the various MTAs, to indirectly inform development of the food contamination annex issued in May 2009.

In two of seven plans, our analysis showed that OPS officials used DHS's CBRN risk assessments to directly inform the plans by modifying planning assumptions contained in the NPS with information obtained from the relevant MTA. OPS officials stated that when they developed the SGS and STRATPLANs, they started by using the planning assumptions from the relevant NPS, as called for in the National Preparedness Guidelines (NPG) and IPS. OPS then used the anthrax and plague MTAs to modify the exposure and casualty estimates for the anthrax and plague annexes. According to OPS officials, they used these MTAs because the information on the consequences of such attacks was more accurate and up to date than the information contained in the NPS.

In four of seven plans, according to OPS officials, the plans were indirectly informed by the planners' knowledge of information contained in the TRAs and MTAs. OPS officials stated that the relevant TRAs and MTAs indirectly informed their planning activities for the Chemical SGS,

[30]For the anthrax and plague annexes to the Biological Attack STRATPLAN, DHS used FOUO versions of the anthrax and plague MTAs from 2008 that included planning assumptions from the respective classified versions of the 2005 anthrax and plague MTAs. The 2008 FOUO MTAs also incorporated consequence estimates produced by HHS officials.

[31]A chemical attack STRATPLAN was not developed prior to planning under HSPD 8 Annex I being put on indefinite hold in July 2009 by the White House National Security Staff pending HSPD 8 revision. The chemical MTAs published prior to the chemical attack SGS include MTAs that address blood agents, nerve agents, pulmonary agents, and vesicants.

Radiological Dispersal and Improvised Nuclear Device STRATPLANs, and food contamination annex. OPS officials said that a range of interagency planners involved in the development of these plans, such as officials from OHA and HHS, were knowledgeable about DHS's CBRN risk assessments and would therefore have indirectly incorporated this information when drafting the plans.

One plan—the foot and mouth disease annex—was not informed by the TRAs or MTAs, according to OPS officials, because DHS's CBRN risk assessments primarily focus on consequences to human health whereas this annex focuses on a foreign animal disease with no significant human health effects. According to officials, this annex was instead based on planning assumptions contained in its associated NPS, as called for by HSPD 8 Annex I, in addition to recommendations from officials with relevant subject matter expertise from the U.S. Department of Agriculture.[32]

Our analysis of a limited set of planning assumptions in the HSPD 8 Annex I plans compared to information contained in the DHS CBRN risk assessments showed that they are generally consistent.[33]

However, as previously noted, DHS officials emphasized that the DHS CBRN risk assessments are just one source of data among many that DHS planners utilize in the course of their planning activities.

---

[32]The foot and mouth disease annex to the Biological STRATPLAN was based on NPS #14 – *Foreign Animal Disease.*

[33]We omitted from this report examples from a limited set of HSPD 8 Annex I planning assumptions compared to CBRN risk assessment content because DHS deemed this information as sensitive or classified.

Neither CBRN Response Plan Developed as Part of the National Response Framework Was Informed by DHS's CBRN Risk Assessments

Neither of the CBRN response plans developed as part of the NRF—the Biological or Nuclear/Radiological Incident Annexes—were informed by DHS's CBRN risk assessments, according to FEMA officials.[34] The NRF was developed to provide the structure and mechanisms for federal support to state and local incident managers for domestic all-hazard events, as called for in Homeland Security Presidential Directive 5 – Management of Domestic Incidents. DHS's Interim National Preparedness Goal of 2005 and related NPG of 2007 state that DHS response plans should incorporate risk assessments. However, according to FEMA officials, the TRAs and MTAs were not used when they revised the Biological and Nuclear/Radiological Incident Annexes. FEMA officials provided multiple reasons for this. First, they noted that these plans are updated versions of the same plans that were originally developed in 2004, before DHS first published its CBRN risk assessments. Second, the FEMA planners responsible for overseeing revision efforts said that they had been unaware of DHS's CBRN risk assessments. Third, according to FEMA officials, even if the FEMA planners had been aware of the TRAs and MTAs, there was no departmental guidance on when or how the CBRN risk assessments should be used when developing such plans (this is discussed in the third objective of this report).

DHS Used Its CBRN Risk Assessments to Directly or Partially Inform Six of Seven of Its CBRN Capabilities

Since 2004, DHS's use of its CBRN risk assessments to inform its CBRN-specific capability investments has varied, from directly impacting its capabilities to not being used at all. Six of the seven CBRN capabilities we examined were informed by DHS's CBRN risk assessments to some extent, according to program officials, DHS documents, and our analysis (see table 4).[35] Our analysis showed that one of the seven capabilities was directly informed by the risk assessments, while our analysis showed or DHS officials told us that five of the seven capabilities were partially

---

[34]The NRF includes seven incident annexes which are to address aspects of how the United States responds to particular types of incidents, two of which are specifically for CBRN threat agents.

[35]For the purposes of this report, we refer to DHS capabilities as being directly informed by DHS's CBRN risk assessments if program managers used the risk assessments to directly align the capability with the threat agents of significant concern and program managers provided us with documentation of these actions. For the purposes of this report, we refer to DHS capabilities as being partially informed by DHS's CBRN risk assessments if program managers told us they used the CBRN risk assessments, as well as other information sources, to inform the development or implementation of the capability.

informed by the risk assessments. However, we could not independently verify this for three of these five capabilities because DHS officials could not document how the risk assessments influenced the capabilities. DHS has developed policies and guidance on the use of risk information for the department's activities, but DHS has not issued guidance to program managers that specifies when or how they should use the CBRN risk assessments to inform CBRN capabilities (this is discussed in the third objective of this report). The DHS Strategic Plan for 2008-2013 states that resource decisions should be informed by relevant risk assessments, but does not provide specific guidance on when or how such decisions should be informed by the department's CBRN risk assessments.[36] Additionally, the Secretary of Homeland Security's March 2011 Management Directive stated that DHS policy is to use risk information and analysis to inform decision making and instructs DHS components to establish mission-appropriate risk management capabilities.[37] See table 4 for a summary of the CBRN capabilities and whether each capability was directly, partially, or not informed by DHS's CBRN risk assessments.

---

[36]Department of Homeland Security, *U.S. Department of Homeland Security Strategic Plan Fiscal Years 2008-2013* (Washington, D.C.: March 2008).

[37]DHS, Integrated Risk Management (Washington, D.C.: March 2011) and DHS, *Risk Management Fundamentals: Homeland Security Risk Management Doctrine* (Washington, D.C.: April 2011).

Table 4: Extent to Which DHS's CBRN Risk Assessments Informed Select DHS CBRN-specific Capabilities

Capability and DHS component	Description of capability	Informed by DHS's CBRN risk assessments[a]
Select chemical capabilities		
Rapidly Deployable Chemical Detection System (RDCDS) *OHA*	A mobile set of chemical air sample collectors designed to dectect chemical threat agents.	Partially
Chemical Security Analysis Center (CSAC) *S&T*	The CSAC works to provide a basis (1) for understanding the risks posed by chemical threat agents and (2) for attr bution associated with their use in a terrorist attack.	Partially
Select biological capabilities		
BioWatch *OHA*	A mobile set of biological air sample collectors designed to detect biological threat agents.	Directly
National Bioforensic Analysis Center (NBFAC) *S&T*	The NBFAC conducts bioforensic analysis of evidence from a biocrime or terrorist attack to attain a "biological fingerprint" to assist investigations.	Partially
National Biosurveillance Integration Center (NBIC) *OHA*	The NBIC works to integrate and analyze information from biosurveillance systems across the federal government, and to disseminate alerts if any biological events are detected.	Partially
Select radiological and nuclear capabilities		
Nuclear Incident Response Teams (NIRT) *FEMA*	The NIRT teams are managed day to day by the Department of Energy and the Environmental Protection Agency. In the event of a high-consequence nuclear incident, the NIRTs fall under FEMA's operational control.	Partially
National Technical Nuclear Forensics Center (NTNFC) *DNDO*	The NTNFC works to advance technical capabilities in the area of predetonation forensics for radiological and nuclear materials and also works to ensure the long-term sustainability of this capability.	No

Source: GAO analysis of DHS documents and information provided by DHS officials.

[a]For the purposes of this report, we define directly informed to mean that program managers used the CBRN risk assessments to directly align the capability with the threat agents of significant concern and program managers provided us with documentation of these actions. We define partially informed to mean that program managers told us they used the CBRN risk assessments, as well as other information sources, to inform the development or implementation of the capability.

Our analysis showed that the extent to which the CBRN capabilities we examined were informed by DHS's CBRN risk assessments varied, but DHS officials described reasons for this variance, as discussed below. In addition, DHS officials noted that basic scientific differences between chemical, biological, and radiological/nuclear threat agents and materials also provide explanations about the differences in how the CBRN risk assessments are used to inform capabilities. For example, DHS officials told us that the relative risk rankings amongst biological agents may be more meaningful than the ranking amongst radiological materials because there are greater differences associated with detecting biological agents, as well as their consequences.

Select DHS Chemical Capabilities

DHS program managers used the risk assessments to partially inform the program management of the RDCDS and the CSAC, as described below. The Director of the CSAC told us that because there are over 13 million possible chemicals that could be considered threat agents, it is impossible to come up with a relative risk ranking of all the chemicals. Therefore, the results of the CTRA are designed to be representative of the highest risk chemical agents and used as a guide—not a definitive resource—for informing capability and planning decisions related to such agents. Additionally, certain chemical compounds have similar enough compositions to be considered together when developing capabilities and response plans.

Rapidly Deployable Chemical Detection System (RDCDS). The OHA Chemical Defense Program used the CTRA to partially inform its RDCDS, according to our analysis as well as DHS officials and documentation. We compared the lists of threat agents that have been programmed to be detected by RDCDS detectors against chemical agents of significant concern in the 2008 and 2010 CTRAs and found that they were generally consistent.[38] The RDCDS program manager told us that the list of threat agents monitored by RDCDS has not changed since 2005 as DHS developed the first and second iterations of the CTRA. However, the program manager told us that when the first CTRA was issued in 2008, program officials reviewed its content to determine whether chemical agents of significant concern in the CTRA were aligned with the chemicals detected by RDCDS. The official said that based on this initial assessment, the RDCDS was generally aligned with the chemical agents of greatest concern.

Chemical Security Analysis Center (CSAC). The Director of the CSAC told us that because a key CSAC mission is to develop the CTRA and the chemical MTAs, these risk assessments are used—to varying extents—to inform the other capabilities that the CSAC maintains. Other capabilities include providing 24/7 technical assistance to other DHS components that

---

[38]We omitted from this report a comparison of RDCDS-detectable threat agents to chemical agents of significant concern in the 2008 and 2010 CTRAs because DHS deemed this information as sensitive or classified.

encounter possible chemical attack situations, such as the National Operations Center. According to the CSAC Director, information from the CTRA is included in the knowledge management system that is used in maintaining this technical assistance capability. However, the CSAC could not provide us with documentation of how it had used the CBRN risk assessments to inform this capability. Further, the CSAC Director told us that the CTRA also informs the CSAC's work in developing models for other DHS components on the effects of certain chemical incidents. We reviewed a CSAC study for the DHS Transportation Security Administration about the release of chemical gases into the atmosphere and found that in the study the CSAC had modeled releases of two different chemical agents, both of which are among the chemical agents of significant concern in the CTRA.

Select DHS Biological Capabilities

We analyzed the extent to which DHS officials used the BTRA and the biological MTAs to inform the program management of three capabilities—BioWatch, the NBFAC, and the NBIC. Our analysis showed that DHS program managers used the risk assessments to either directly inform (BioWatch) or partially inform (NBFAC and NBIC) their decisions, as described below. The program manager of BioWatch told us that it makes sense for the program to use the most reliable tool available to them—in this case, the CBRN risk assessments—to determine what agents to program into their detection system. The director of the NBFAC told us that the BTRA was used on one occasion to directly inform program management and prioritization. The NBIC branch chief told us that the BTRA is used at a strategic level and that the center's staff is very familiar with the contents of the BTRA and the biological MTAs. However, he stated that the NBIC's mission is to monitor detection efforts for all biological agents, particularly emerging infectious diseases, and to provide alerts about potentially dangerous biological incidents to state and local homeland security professionals. Therefore, the NBIC branch chief said that the relative risk ranking of a given biological agent would not be an appropriate basis for the prioritization of resources at the operational level.

BioWatch. We found that the BioWatch program was generally consistent with the biological agents of significant concern identified in the BTRA. DHS documents state that the BTRA is to be used to update the list of threat agents monitored by BioWatch. DHS deployed BioWatch in

2003, before the release of the first BTRA in 2006.[39] Since then, DHS has reprogrammed BioWatch detection efforts once, in response to the 2006 BTRA. The BioWatch program manager told us that they review each iteration of the BTRA to ensure that the BioWatch program is aligned with the biological agents of significant concern. We compared the lists of threat agents that have been programmed to be detected by the BioWatch program since 2006 against the biological agents of significant concern in the 2006, 2008, and 2010 BTRAs and found them generally consistent.[40]

The BioWatch program manager also told us that future generations of BioWatch are being developed to detect a larger number of biological threat agents. According to BioWatch documents, these agents are to be determined by the BTRA's risk rankings. OHA officials told us they use the BTRA to inform BioWatch because it is the most relevant CBRN risk assessment available to them and because it allows OHA to focus BioWatch detection efforts on the biological agents of significant concern.

National Bioforensic Analysis Center (NBFAC). We found that the NBFAC used the CBRN risk assessments to partially inform its capabilities. Officials from NBFAC told us that the center used information from the BTRA to inform its priorities for developing tools needed to support their work in biological forensic attribution. Our analysis showed that the NBFAC's forensic attribution capabilities were generally consistent with the biological agents of significant concern in the BTRA.[41] However, NBFAC officials stated that because the NBFAC is mandated to maintain capabilities for other biological materials, including biological agents that are not considered high risk, future BTRA results would not necessarily lead to reprioritization of NBFAC's attribution capability development efforts.

---

[39]For more information on BioWatch and DHS's biosurveillance efforts, see GAO, *Biosurveillance: Efforts to Develop a National Biosurveillance Capability Need a National Strategy and a Designated Leader,* GAO-10-645 (Washington, D.C.: June 30, 2010).

[40]We omitted from this report a comparison of BioWatch-detectable threat agents to the biological agents of significant concern in the 2006, 2008, and 2010 BTRAs because DHS deemed this information as sensitive or classified.

[41]We omitted from this report a comparison of agents for which the NBFAC has developed attribution capabilities to the biological agents of significant concern in the 2006, 2008, and 2010 BTRAs because DHS deemed this information as sensitive or classified.

National Biosurveillance Integration Center (NBIC). We found that the NBIC used the CBRN risk assessments to partially inform its activities. According to the OHA branch chief responsible for the NBIC, NBIC personnel are aware of the information in DHS's CBRN risk assessments and consider this information at a strategic level. However, the NBIC could not provide us with documentation of how it had used the CBRN risk assessments to inform its capabilities at the strategic level. The NBIC branch chief also stated that NBIC does not use information from the BTRA or biological MTAs at an operational level to inform the management of their capability. The official provided documentation showing that the NBIC's mission is to collect and integrate information about biological agent detection from a variety of federal government detection systems.[42] The OHA branch chief stated that because the NBIC's mission is to integrate and provide alerts on all biological agents, including emerging and infectious diseases that are not included in the CBRN risk assessments, it is not relevant whether the biological agents the NBIC is monitoring are considered to be high risk according to the BTRA or the MTAs, although these agents are also monitored.

Select DHS Radiological and Nuclear Capabilities

Our analysis showed that DHS program managers' use of the risk assessments to inform radiological and nuclear capabilities varied from partially informing their decisions to not informing their decision at all. Officials from the NTNFC told us that because of the relatively small universe of radiological and nuclear materials, the risk rankings among these materials did not matter as much as the relative threat and consequence information for biological and chemical agents. Additionally, DHS officials told us the challenges that first responders would face in responding to a nuclear explosion in a city may be a more important concern than the type of threat material used in such an attack.

Nuclear Incident Response Teams (NIRTs). FEMA officials told us that information from the R/NTRA appendix to the 2008 ITRA partially informed the program management of the NIRTs and FEMA's other

---

[42]The NBIC was created under the Implementing Recommendations of the 9/11 Commission Act of 2007. Pub. L. No. 110-53, § 1101, 121 Stat. 266, 375 (2007) (codified at 6 U.S.C. § 195b). NBIC is to help provide early detection and situational awareness of biological threats by integrating information and supporting the interagency biosurveillance community. For more information, see our report: *Biosurveillance: Developing a Collaboration Strategy Is Essential to Fostering Interagency Data and Resource Sharing*, GAO-10-171 (Washington, D.C.: December 2009).

nuclear response capabilities. Specifically, FEMA officials said that information in the R/NTRA appendix, among other sources, was used to inform FEMA's IND Response and Recovery Program.[43] Starting in 2010, FEMA officials said that NIRT-related activities were aligned with the IND Response and Recovery Program. FEMA officials told us that because of this, their management of the NIRTs is partially informed, by extension, by the R/NTRA appendix. However, FEMA could not provide us with documentation of how it specifically had used the R/NTRA appendix to inform the NIRTs.

National Technical Nuclear Forensics Center (NTNFC). An NTNFC official told us that the NTNFC did not use information contained in the R/NTRA appendix to the 2008 ITRA, and the NTNFC does not intend to use the 2011 R/NTRA (once published) to inform its activities. The same official told us that these CBRN risk assessments do not provide useful information to inform NTNFC activities because nuclear forensic capabilities are developed for all radiological and nuclear materials, regardless of their relative risk. Further, he stated that NTNFC is already aware of the universe of possible radiological and nuclear materials that could be used to attack the nation. DHS S&T's Chief Medical and Science Advisor, the official who oversees the development of DHS's CBRN risk assessments, agreed that NTNFC's capabilities need to be able to identify all radiological and nuclear materials, and that therefore the CBRN risk assessments were not relevant for NTNFC's efforts.

---

[43]This program identified IND response capability gaps at the federal, state, and local levels and reported these gaps in the *DHS Strategy for Improving the National Response and Recovery from an IND Attack* (Washington, D.C.: April 2010). FEMA is currently drafting an implementation plan for this strategy, which is intended to identify approaches to narrowing these gaps by further developing nuclear response capabilities across the nation.

Specific Guidance Not Established to Help Ensure DHS's CBRN Risk Assessments Are Used to Inform Its Response Plans and Capabilities

DHS policy states that DHS components should use risk assessment information to inform planning and capability investment decisions, but DHS has not established specific guidance, such as written procedures, that details when and how DHS components should consider using the department's CBRN-specific risk assessments to inform such activities.[44] According to the National Strategy for Homeland Security of 2007, the assessment and management of risk underlies all homeland security activities, including decisions about when, where, and how to invest in resources—including planning and capabilities—that eliminate, control, or mitigate risks. The TRAs and MTAs—the department's most CBRN-specific risk assessments—were used to inform to varying extents 9 of 12 response plans and 6 of 7 capabilities we analyzed, and how the risk assessments were used to inform these plans and capabilities varied. DHS officials told us that while DHS policy calls for the use of risk information to inform the department's activities, no DHS guidance specifically requires DHS officials to use the TRAs and MTAs for CBRN planning and capability investments or explains how officials should use the risk assessments to inform their decision making. As a result, the CBRN risk assessments were used to varying extents and in varying ways by DHS components for the plans and capabilities we analyzed. DHS officials said that they considered the risk assessments but chose not to use them to inform one of the plans and one of the capabilities we reviewed because they were not useful for the plan or the capability. In addition, the risk assessments were not considered at all for two of the plans we reviewed.

Since at least 2007, DHS has emphasized the need to incorporate risk information derived from risk assessments into departmental activities, and since 2009 DHS has issued a range of guidance—including an interim framework, a policy memo, a management directive, and a doctrine—on the use of such risk information. Specifically, DHS's Interim Integrated Risk Management Framework of January 2009 identified risk assessments as a fundamental information source for risk-informed decision making and noted that the BTRA and CTRA are examples of risk assessments produced by the department that can be used to inform risk

---

[44]DHS's Interim National Preparedness Goal of 2005 and related National Preparedness Guidelines of 2007 state that DHS response plans should be informed by threat analysis and risk assessment information. Further, DHS's 2008-2013 Strategic Plan states that because the homeland security mission is complex and resources are constrained, the department will use risk assessments to inform resource decisions.

management efforts.[45] In May 2010, the Secretary of Homeland Security issued a policy memo that requires, among other things, the use of risk assessments to inform decision making and the establishment of mechanisms for sharing risk assessments with relevant stakeholders. In March 2011, as called for in the Secretary's memo, DHS issued a management directive on integrated risk management at the department.[46] This management directive, among other things, tasks the Director of the Office of Risk Management and Analysis (RMA) within DHS's NPPD with establishing a system to facilitate the sharing of risk analysis and data across the department.[47] Further, in April 2011, DHS issued its doctrine for risk management—titled Risk Management Fundamentals—the first in a series of publications that RMA plans to issue to provide a structured approach for the distribution and employment of risk information and analysis efforts across the department.[48]

DHS's existing guidance on risk management generally identifies the importance of using risk assessments to inform departmental decision making, but it does not specifically address when and how particular risk assessments—including the TRAs and MTAs—should be considered for use by departmental entities for planning and capability investment purposes. DHS officials stated that more specific guidance has not been developed by the department or its components and agencies because they were not required to do so. However, *Standards for Internal Control in the Federal Government* state that officials should take actions, such as establishing written procedures, to help ensure that management's

---

[45]DHS, *Interim Integrated Risk Management Framework* (Washington, D.C.: January 2009). This interim framework was replaced by DHS's *Risk Management Fundamentals: Homeland Security Risk Management Doctrine* in April 2011.

[46]DHS, Management Directive 007-03: *Integrated Risk Management* (Washington, D.C.: March 2011).

[47]According to RMA officials, at the completion of our review RMA was in the process of drafting instructions for implementation of Management Directive 007-03, including the operations of the DHS Risk Steering Committee. The DHS Risk Steering Committee is to serve as the governance structure to ensure collaboration and information-sharing for risk management and analysis across the department. RMA officials told us they expected to complete these instructions by late 2011.

[48]DHS, *Risk Management Fundamentals: Homeland Security Risk Management Doctrine* (Washington, D.C.: April 2011). Risk Management Fundamentals replaced DHS's Interim Risk Management Framework of 2009.

directives are carried out.[49,50] In addition, DHS's *Interim Integrated Risk Management Framework* of January 2009 stated that DHS must establish processes that make risk information available among the department and its components and agencies when and where it is needed, noting that the ability to receive and provide meaningful and usable risk information in a timely manner requires well coordinated and established processes.

While DHS has issued guidance that generally states that risk assessments should be used to inform departmental activities, DHS could better help to ensure that its relevant CBRN-specific risk assessments—the TRAs and MTAs—are considered for use in informing CBRN-specific planning and capability investments if more specific guidance requiring such consideration is established. DHS officials also stated that establishing written procedures for such consideration could better help to ensure that officials responsible for CBRN response planning and capability investment decision making consider the CBRN risk assessments as a means to obtain current risk information for specific CBRN threat agents. This information could be used to inform the planning assumptions that CBRN response plans are designed to address, as well as the requirements development process for CBRN capabilities. In addition, DHS officials noted that the lack of written procedures requiring DHS officials to consider using the TRAs and MTAs to inform DHS's CBRN plans and capabilities could negatively affect the likelihood that future DHS officials consider using the risk assessments when planning and making investment decisions. By establishing more specific guidance that details when and how DHS components should consider using the TRAs and MTAs to inform CBRN plans and capabilities, DHS would be better positioned to ensure that officials consider and, as appropriate, incorporate the department's most detailed CBRN-specific risk information. As a result, DHS would be better positioned to ensure that its CBRN response plans and capabilities align with the assumptions and results contained within the TRAs and MTAs.

---

[49]GAO/AIMD-00-21.3.1.

[50]Further, internal control activities are an integral part of an entity's planning, implementing, reviewing, and accountability for stewardship of government resources and achieving effective results.

Conclusions

The anthrax attacks of 2001 raised concerns that the United States is vulnerable to terrorist attacks using CBRN agents. Since 2001, DHS has developed a range of CBRN risk assessments, response plans, and related capabilities to prepare for such attacks. DHS has spent at least $70 million developing these risk assessments. Using its CBRN risk assessments to help inform CBRN response planning and capability investments is consistent with DHS policy and could help to better ensure that relevant information contained in the risk assessments is used to inform such plans and capabilities. Further, given that there are thousands of CBRN agents that could potentially pose a risk to the nation in an era of declining federal budgets and constrained resources, the federal government must ensure that it is focusing its limited resources on preparing to respond to the highest risk agents. Without procedures for using the risk assessments to inform capability investment decision making, use of the assessments for such decisions may continue to vary or not occur at all. More specific guidance on when and how DHS officials should consider using the department's CBRN risk assessments to inform planning and investments could better help to ensure their consistent use and that this use is sustained beyond the tenure of any given agency official.

Recommendation for Executive Action

To better ensure the consistent use of DHS's CBRN risk assessments at the department's components and agencies, we recommend that the Secretary of Homeland Security:

- Establish more specific guidance, including written procedures, that details when and how DHS components should consider using the department's CBRN risk assessments to inform related response plan and capability investment decision making.

Agency Comments

We received written comments on the draft report, which are reproduced in full in appendix I. DHS also provided technical comments, which were incorporated as appropriate. DHS concurred with the basis for the recommendation and discussed an action that S&T—which is responsible for developing the department's CBRN risk assessments—plans to take to address the recommendation. Specifically, DHS noted that it is currently developing user guidelines for its CBRN risk assessments. In addition, DHS also stated that S&T is committed to continuing to work with relevant stakeholders to ensure that its risk assessments are useful for informing response planning and capability investment decision making.

We are sending copies of this report to the Secretary of Homeland Security, appropriate congressional committees, and other interested parties. The report also is available at no charge on the GAO website at http://www.gao.gov.

If you or your staff have any further questions about this report, please contact me at (202) 512-8777 or jenkinswo@gao.gov. Contact points for our Offices of Congressional Relations and Public Affairs may be found on the last page of this report. Key contributors to this report are listed in appendix II.

William O. Jenkins, Jr.
Director, Homeland Security and Justice Issues

Appendix I: Comments from the Department of Homeland Security

U.S. Department of Homeland Security
Washington, D.C. 20528

Homeland Security

October 6, 2011

William O. Jenkins, Jr.
Director, Homeland Security and Justice Issues
U.S. Government Accountability Office
441 G Street, NW
Washington, DC 20548

Re: Draft Report ███████████████████████████████
        ████████████████████

Dear Mr. Jenkins:

Thank you for the opportunity to review and comment on this draft report. The U.S. Department of Homeland Security (DHS) appreciates the U.S. Government Accountability Office's (GAO's) work in planning and conducting its review and issuing this report. The Department is pleased to note the report's positive acknowledgement that DHS has coordinated with other federal departments in developing Chemical, Biological, Radiological, and Nuclear (CBRN) Risk Assessments.

The draft report contained one recommendation directed to DHS, with which the Department concurs, as discussed below. Specifically, to better ensure consistent use of the Department's CBRN Risk Assessments at DHS Components and agencies, GAO recommends that the Secretary of Homeland Security:

Recommendation: Establish more specific guidance, including written procedures, that details when and how DHS components should consider using the department's CBRN Risk Assessments to inform related response plans and capability investment decision-making.

Response: Concur. The Department's Science and Technology Directorate, Chemical and Biological Defense Division (CBD) is committed to continuing its work with DHS's Office of Infrastructure Protection, Office of Health Affairs, and others to ensure that CBRN Risk Assessments take stakeholders' needs into consideration during Assessment development and, upon completion, are useful for informing response planning and capability investment decision making. In addition to seeking stakeholder input on the Assessments during development, CBD is in the process of developing user guidelines to be submitted with completed CBRN Risk Assessments. These guidelines will maximize the utility of the Assessments and provide helpful resources to ensure appropriate interpretation and extrapolation of the information contained in the Risk documents.

Again, thank you for the opportunity to review and comment on this draft report. Sensitivity and technical comments were provided under separate cover. We look forward to working with you on future Homeland Security issues.

Sincerely,

Jim H. Crumpacker
Director
Departmental GAO-OIG Liaison Office

2

Appendix II: GAO Contacts and Staff Acknowledgments

GAO Contacts	William O. Jenkins, (202) 512-8777 or jenkinswo@gao.gov
Staff Acknowledgments	In addition to the contact named above, Edward George (Assistant Director), David Lysy (Analyst-in-Charge), David Schneider, Bonnie Doty, David Alexander, Tracey King, and Katherine Davis made key contributions to this report.

Related GAO Products

National Preparedness: DHS and HHS Can Further Strengthen Coordination for Chemical, Biological, Radiological, and Nuclear Risk Assessments. GAO-11-606. Washington, D.C.: June 21, 2011.

Public Health Preparedness: Developing and Acquiring Medical Countermeasures Against Chemical, Biological, Radiological, and Nuclear Agents. GAO-11-567T. Washington, D.C.: April 13, 2011.

Measuring Disaster Preparedness: FEMA Has Made Limited Progress in Assessing National Capabilities. GAO-11-260T. Washington, D.C.: March 17, 2011.

Biosurveillance: Efforts to Develop a National BioSurveillance Capability Need a National Strategy and a Designated Leader. GAO-10-645. Washington, D.C.: June 30, 2010.

Homeland Defense: DOD Can Enhance Efforts to Identify Capabilities to Support Civil Authorities during Disasters. GAO-10-386. Washington, D.C.: March 30, 2010.

Combating Nuclear Terrorism: Actions Needed to Better Prepare to Recover from Possible Attacks Using Radiological or Nuclear Materials. GAO-10-204. Washington, D.C.: January 29, 2010.

Biosurveillance: Developing a Collaboration Strategy Is Essential to Fostering Interagency Data and Resource Sharing. GAO-10-171. Washington, D.C.: December 18, 2009.

Homeland Defense: Planning, Resourcing, and Training Issues Challenge DOD's Response to Domestic Chemical, Biological, Radiological, Nuclear, and High-Yield Explosive Incidents. GAO-10-123. Washington, D.C.: October 7, 2009.

Homeland Defense: Preliminary Observations on Defense Chemical, Biological, Radiological, Nuclear, and High-Yield Explosives Consequence Management Plans and Preparedness. GAO-09-927T. Washington, D.C.: July 28, 2009.

Project BioShield Act: HHS Has Supported Development, Procurement, and Emergency Use of Medical Countermeasures to Address Health Threats. GAO-09-878R. Washington, D.C.: July 24, 2009.

Project BioShield: HHS Can Improve Agency Internal Controls for Its New Contracting Authorities. GAO-09-820. Washington, D.C.: July 21, 2009.

National Preparedness: FEMA Has Made Progress, but Needs to Complete and Integrate Planning, Exercise, and Assessment Efforts. GAO-09-369. Washington, D.C.: April 30, 2009.

Homeland Security: First Responders' Ability to Detect and Model Hazardous Releases in Urban Areas is Significantly Limited. GAO-08-180. Washington, D.C.: June 27, 2008.

Risk Management: Strengthening the Use of Risk Management Principles in Homeland Security. GAO-08-904T. Washington, D.C.: June 25, 2008.

Emergency Management: Observations on DHS's Preparedness for Catastrophic Disasters. GAO-08-868T. Washington, D.C.: June 11, 2008.

Highlights of a Forum: Strengthening the Use of Risk Management Principles in Homeland Security. GAO-08-627SP. Washington, D.C.: April 15, 2008.

Project BioShield: Actions Needed to Avoid Repeating Past Problems with Procuring New Anthrax Vaccine and Managing the Stockpile of Licensed Vaccine. GAO-08-88. Washington, D.C.: October 23, 2007.

Homeland Security: Applying Risk Management Principles to Guide Federal Investments. GAO-07-386T. Washington, D.C.: February 7, 2007.

Chemical and Biological Defense: Management Actions Are Needed to Close the Gap Between Army Chemical Unit Preparedness and State National Priorities. GAO-07-143. Washington, D.C.: January 19, 2007.

Risk Management: Further Refinements Needed to Assess Risk and Prioritize Protective Measures at Ports and Other Critical Infrastructure. GAO-06-91. Washington, D.C.: December 15, 2005.

Internal Control: Standards for Internal Control in the Federal Government. GAO/AIMD-00-21.3.1. Washington, D.C.: November 1, 1999.